Catherine,

On this Valentine's Day
and through all the
seasons of our lives,

I give you my heart...
I give you my love...

PASSIONATE
HEARTS

PASSIONATE HEARTS

*the poetry of
sexual love*

AN ANTHOLOGY
COMPILED AND EDITED BY
WENDY MALTZ

NEW WORLD LIBRARY
NOVATO, CALIFORNIA

New World Library
14 Pamaron Way
Novato, CA 94949

Cover and text design: Mary Ann Casler
Cover photograph: Paul Dahlquist
Editorial: Becky Benenate

Library of Congress Cataloging-in-Publication Data

Passionate hearts : the poetry of sexual love / edited by Wendy Maltz
: preface by Molly Peacock.
p.   cm.
ISBN 1-57731-007-1 (cloth)
ISBN 1-57731-122-1 (paperback : alk. paper)
1. Erotic poetry.   2. Love poetry.   I. Maltz, Wendy.
PN6110.E65P37   96-31046
808.81'93538--dc20   CIP

First hardcover printing, December 1996
First paperback printing, January 2000
Printed in Canada on acid-free paper
Distributed to the trade by Publishers Group West

10 9 8 7 6 5

To Larry, my Love

CONTENTS

CONTENTS

CHAPTER THREE
varied dances
91

CHAPTER FOUR
deeper intimacies
133

CHAPTER FIVE
graceful transformations
169

CONTENTS

PREFACE

by molly peacock

This is a book of passion. Take it to bed with you. Curl up with it alone — or with another passionate heart. This is a book of poems that put the ancient wisdom of the body into words. It is full of the little miracles of understanding that only poets know how to make.

As we perceive through our tongues, noses, skin, ears, and eyes, we learn to delight in the world. But sometimes our deepest physical responses are so strong and connected with our emotions, we hardly know how to convey them in words. That is where poetry comes in, and where Wendy Maltz, the editor of this collection, has worked her wizardry.

As a healer, she appreciates how poetry can universalize our experience simply by being so intimate, and she has searched beyond the predictable choices for *Passionate*

Hearts: The Poetry of Sexual Love. Discovering gems of poetry by emerging writers as well as established ones, she has grouped them to show us how to feel our way through sensual experience within an intimate relationship.

Of all the freedoms of the late 20th century, my favorite is how explicit poets can be. They can take timeless themes and deliver them to us with the images and associations of right now. In this way poets are the truth tellers of the cultural body. Here, in this collection, they uncover erotic truths and supply us with metaphors that heal as well as reveal: bold, positive, direct language for sexual sharing.

Each of us is capable of passion, but the poems gathered here *kindle* passion. As they touch us, they deepen our capacities for touch.

INTRODUCTION

*"What sex is, we don't know, but it must be some sort
of fire. For it always communicates a sense of warmth,
of glow. And when the glow becomes a pure shine, then
we feel the sense of beauty."*

— D. H. LAWRENCE

This book of poetry has come about through my quest
to unlock the mystery of sexual love. This is not a new
quest for me. It's a search I've been on, in some fashion, for
most of my life. As a sex therapist, I've made a profession
of understanding and explaining sex.

As a young child, I remember repeatedly harassing my
parents with question after question about sex. Their
answers changed over time, becoming more specific and
elaborate as I grew more mature and inquisitive. By the
time I was eleven, budding with my own sexual feelings,
curious about true love, and frustrated with technical
sounding sperm and egg explanations, I pressed them for

more information about the act itself. "The woman lies on her back with her legs in the air and arms open, and the man lies on top of her...." Although my parents continued talking, I heard only an occasional word after this opening line. I was stunned. The image that formed in my mind was of dead bugs on the sidewalk — lying with their feet in the air, tangled together, and parched by the sun. My first explicit sexual image was a major disappointment. Why would anyone want to share an experience like that with someone they love?

For each of us, our concept of sexual love has been shaped over many years by the sexual images permitted and promoted in our culture. Today, it's hard not to find images of sex in our society. Since the dawn of the sexual revolution in the 1960s, we have stripped away the old, puritanical restrictions that once made sex a taboo subject. Erotic images are woven so extensively into every aspect of our culture that they leap out at us when we open a magazine, turn on the television set, settle back in a movie theater, or pass a billboard on the freeway. It is sad and ironic that while our sexually obsessed culture feeds us a steady stream of arousing sexual images, many of us feel starved when it comes to understanding or sharing sexual love.

Very few of the unabashedly graphic images we see daily depict adults engaged in what we would describe as *healthy sexual intimacy*. Though many of us desire meaningful, intimate connection with a lover, most of the sexual images we are exposed to condition us to be aroused to sex *without* love. Like someone who has eaten only junk food, we wind up feeling malnourished. No amount of binges on "junk sex" can satisfy our hunger for real connection. In our enthusiasm to overcome puritanical constraints, perhaps we overlooked the importance of promoting certain kinds of sex over others.

Sexual interaction based on mutual caring and respect is very different from sex in which people are objectified or exploited. Loving, intimate sex can be far more enjoyable and satisfying than impersonal sex. But to enjoy these pleasures of sexual love we need to know more.

Although we are naturally wired with a strong sexual drive, we are not born knowing all the information we need to fully understand it. Most of us have questions about sex. But in our culture, the answers are not always accessible or complete. To explore our potential as sexual beings, we need to understand not only the mechanics of sex, but also the interpersonal context for enjoying sexual love. We need more images that give us models for healthy relating. With exposure to these images we can learn that healthy intimacy is arousing and intensely pleasurable. Instead of a cultural diet of "junk sex" that leaves us titillated, but starved, we need lasting, nourishing ways to satisfy our hunger for sexual connection.

My quest for understanding sexual intimacy took a more serious turn when I began treating adult survivors of sexual abuse. Many of these people suffered from crippling sexual fears and dangerous sexual compulsions. For them, sex was often unpleasant at best. Their sexual relations left them feeling emotionally isolated, or out of control. *Healthy sexual intimacy* was an oxymoron. They could not conceptualize it, even when I explained that it was defined by concrete conditions: Consent. Equality. Respect. Trust. Safety.

About five years ago, my long quest for understanding sexual love became more focused. I began an ardent search to find positive sexual images. I wanted healthy alternatives to the negative images that surround us in our culture, so that I could show those who have felt confused about or hurt by sex that it can be very different, that it can even inspire moments of beauty.

This is a message all of us need to hear, throughout our lives. As a parent, I want my children to have healthy sexual models to learn from as they grow older. All of our children deserve to know about the importance of sexual health and the possibilities for joy and pleasure that sex affords. As an intimate partner, I want to be reminded of the infinite dimensions my husband and I can explore in heart-connected sex. All of us who are in long-term relationships need more resources to draw inspiration from, whether we are just setting out as a young couple or growing older with a partner.

To begin, I scoured films, video selections, popular books, and magazines for images that portrayed sex as mutually enjoyable, socially responsible, and physically safe. I was shocked at how few sexually explicit examples of healthy sex I could find. The images I found — perfume ads, greeting cards, and modern love stories — were pretty weak stuff compared to the latest issue of *Penthouse* magazine. Although there were some passages in erotica and romance novels that conveyed healthy sex dynamics, many of the themes in these stories still centered on impersonal, irresponsible, or secretive sex.

Next, my search took me to the library. Perhaps the

joys of mutually satisfying sexual love had been celebrated by writers years ago. I began sifting through classic works of literature and poetry. But these works, by and large, let me down. I found an occasional gem, but more often I was reminded of the long history of sexual inequality between men and women from which we are still evolving. Older poems too often lacked the mutually intimate love that a healthy, mature relationship demands.

Until quite recently, male poets have dominated this genre. Too many of the erotic poems I found in the classic texts tended to repeat themes of objectifying, adoring, or controlling females. *The Kama Sutra*, one of the classic Eastern love texts, speaks repeatedly of intimate relations between "the girl" and "the man." In a chapter entitled "Creating Confidence in the Girl," the text advises the man whose young lover is reluctant:

> *". . . if she would not yield to him he should frighten her by saying 'I shall impress marks of my teeth and nails on your lips and breasts . . .'"*[1]

Classic Western love poems are generally less graphically direct, but often just as offensive to my ethic of

---

[1] Sir Richard Burton, *The Illustrated Kama Sutra* (Rochester, VT: Park Street Press, 1991), p. 24.

healthy intimacy. They perpetuated the cultural norms of their day, especially the belief that a woman's personal sexual experience was irrelevant; her pleasure would come in being a submissive vehicle for satisfying a man's sexual desires. In "The Jewels," the French poet Charles Baudelaire writes:

> My well-beloved was stripped. Knowing my whim
> She wore her tinkling gems, but naught besides;
> And showed such pride as, while her luck betides,
> A sultan's favoured slave may show to him.[2]

In classic poetry, true consent, based on a right to refuse sex at any time, seemed nonexistent. William Butler Yeats describes a man asserting power over his lover in "Down by the Salley Gardens":

> She bid me take love easy, as the leaves grow on
> the tree
> But I, being young and foolish, with her would
> not agree.[3]

Sometimes I found a poem that seemed to honor the

---

[2]Jon Stallworthy, ed. *A Book of Love Poetry* (New York: Oxford University Press, 1974), p. 170.
[3]*The Collected Poems of W.B. Yeats* (New York: Macmillan, 1956), p. 20.

importance of mutuality in intimacy. But then I would hear something in it that echoed back to an imbalance of power. In "Invitation to the Voyage," Baudelaire begins to weave more appropriate imagery about making time to savor sexual pleasure:

> *Imagine the magic*
> *of living together*
> *there, with all the time in the world*
> *for loving each other, . . .*[4]

But within a few lines, he refers to his lover as "my sister, my child." I shuddered to think how survivors of incest and rape would respond to the specific images I was finding, and how all of us would hear the wrong message reinforced, if I were to return to these poets for inspiration. I felt disillusioned that the traditional "love" poets whose works I had enjoyed 25 years ago, when I studied poetry in college, were reinforcing relationship dynamics that prevent mutually rewarding sexual love and intimacy. However lyrical or sensuous the language sounds, love poetry of the past lacks a foundation of equality between two partners. Without this framework, even the most

---

[4]Peter Washington, ed. *Erotic Poems* (New York: Alfred Knopf, 1994), p. 26.

beautiful poem fails to evoke relationships built on mutual caring, with both partners active participants in loving.

Even though my initial efforts to find sex-positive imagery uncovered only a handful of appropriate works, this step in my search was important. It got me reading and appreciating poetry.

Poetry speaks a universal language. Unlike longer prose, which tends to relate more specifically to a character, poems evoke images that resonate for each of us, regardless of gender or sexual orientation. With a few spare lines of text, they capture a world of experience. We don't need an advanced degree in literature to appreciate the meaning of a well-written poem. The words speak right to our heart. The poet's metaphors connect our actions as humans with the larger life forces in nature. And they focus on the momentary glimpses we gain through experience. Because sex itself is a momentary but profound experience, poetry is a perfect medium for exploring the meaning, mystery, and beauty of sex.

Out of the disappointment of my initial search came my strong conviction to create a resource for positive images of sexual love. I would locate the elusive images myself. And I would do it with quality, readable poetry.

Accessible to anyone.

I launched a campaign to locate the works of contemporary poets writing about sexual love. I thought perhaps they, writing in today's more egalitarian era, would be a better source for works. I sought "heartcore" poems; poems that inspire and celebrate healthy sexual intimacy; poems in which heart connection is at the core of the sexual experience. I advertised in national poetry journals, sent flyers to creative writing centers and writing programs at universities, and began making personal contacts with some influential contemporary poets.

As I reviewed the more than 1,500 submissions, I kept in mind that each poem had to meet the conditions that I consider necessary for healthy sexual intimacy. I asked: Does this poem represent mutual caring and desire? Do the partners relate as equals, respecting each other as separate individuals? Is there a sense of emotional trust and honesty? Are the sexual interactions assumed to be safe from emotional and physical harm? Does the poem celebrate sensual pleasures?

When these conditions are met in life, as in poetry, we are free to enjoy and explore sexual love. Honoring healthy sex conditions allows us to safely embrace sex, enjoy it, without fear of any negative outcomes. Only good will result. Adopting these guidelines does not restrict intimate sexual pleasure, but rather permits it to grow and flourish.

My search into contemporary poetry brought personal satisfaction and rich rewards. I began to discover that today's poets are very interested in helping to explain and explore sexual love. For the general reader, the words are understandable. For the reader with a deeper background in literature, the poems bring together some well-known contemporary poets, and some newer voices. Together, their combined perspectives deeply penetrate the mystery of sex.

Listen to Molly Peacock, in "The Purr," searching for new words to describe the same mystery that D. H. Lawrence could not solve:

> *. . . The mysterious thrum*
> *that science can't yet explain awakes a hum*
> *in me, the sound something numb come alive makes.*

And poet Sharon Olds gives new meaning to familiar words as she describes "making love" in her poem, "The Knowing":

> *... For an hour*
> *we wake and doze, and slowly I know*
> *that though we are sated, though we are hardly*
> *touching, this is the coming the other*
> *brought us to the edge of — we are entering,*
> *deeper and deeper, gaze by gaze,*
> *this place beyond the other places,*
> *beyond the body itself, we are making*
> *love.*

When I read Stephen Corey's "Complicated Shadows," in which he recalls a sexual experience outdoors on a hot day, I couldn't help but smile remembering my childhood image of insect sex. In Corey's very different view, the image came wonderfully alive with new consciousness about the interplay and union of two lovers:

> *To hawks we're a woodland insect,*
> *four legs above and four below, twitching*
> *on the ground ...*
> *... We are weaving and folding, we*
> *know this soil is a great compost heap,*
> *we are making and unmaking*
> *light — forcing the aging hot sun to run.*

The poems I have selected for this volume celebrate the positive aspects of sex, built on a platform of healthy relating. As these poets illustrate so well, we have no need to feel shame about sex. It's as natural to us as laughter. When the conditions are right — when we're feeling safe and not humiliated — laughter bubbles up as a wonderful energy between two people. It feels good. And it's the same with sex. Appropriately, many of the poems are light-hearted and playful. Allison Joseph, in "Learning to Laugh," describes how lovemaking can bring forth laughter so rich "that I couldn't believe such a sound/ could come from my naked body." Yet, she goes on to tell of:

> ... the laughs that just keep
> coming, rising out of me
> to stop traffic on the boulevard,
> drivers slowing to listen
> to the most joy they've ever heard.

The organization for this book grew naturally out of the poems themselves. By an almost organic process, it seemed that they fit together into chapters about the stages of human sexual relating.

As I organized the poems, I realized that the shape of the book was a metaphor in itself. In sex, we begin with desire and excitement; build to a plateau; experience the release of orgasm; then move on to a state of resolution. This is the physical description we understand as the sexual response cycle. In many ways, this act of sexual expression recapitulates all the stages of healthy sexual relating.

In a relationship, we experience the building excitement of getting to know a potential partner. The opening chapter, "Tender Awakenings," contains poems that explore that first spark of initial attraction. These poets write about the fears and hesitancies that sometimes get in the way of our desire for love. They describe the importance of waiting until both partners are ready. They help us to understand the foundation of trust and safety we need for awakening to shared sexual pleasure.

Once both partners feel ready, they can move forward to share the playfulness and sensuality of physical love. The second chapter, "Passionate Pleasures," explores some of the infinite ways that two bodies, two hearts, might intertwine as one. These poems celebrate the intensity and ecstasy that come from physical sharing. This is frightening, at times, to the people in these poems, just as it can be overwhelming in real life. Sexual arousal brings with it the experience of abandon. Surrendering to sexual pleasure challenges our basic human instinct to be alert and in control of ourselves. In this chapter, couples work through their fears to savor sexual sharing and the lasting connection it brings them.

As a relationship progresses, partners build a platform on which different dances and expressions occur. In the third chapter, "Varied Dances," we see sex explored in all sorts of settings. The poets show us how to tackle the challenges of a long-term relationship. How do we remain sexual when beset by boredom, stress, disappointments, children at the door? How do we rekindle the spark that attracted us in the first place? How shall we seduce the partner we know so well?

In "Deeper Intimacies," the fourth chapter, we see the possibilities for what might happen when a couple remains together and remains sexual for a long time. The poets show us how vulnerable we are when we truly open ourselves to another, yet how vast the opportunities are when we take that risk. The depth of emotional intimacy builds, generating peak experiences. These poems describe moments of conscious loving, in which the self and the partner are revealed.

For those who have nurtured a healthy relationship for a long time, the final phase can transform a sexual relationship into something almost spiritual. If we are lucky enough to enjoy a long, healthy relationship with the same partner, the natural aging process kicks in. Yet, even in our youth-conscious culture, some couples are wise enough to see beyond the wrinkles and graying hair, and savor the sexual energy that remains.

Even as these energies decline with age, these couples celebrate the moments they have left together. The memories of all that has passed between them take on a substance that counterbalances time's physical losses. In "Orchestration," Jane Mayes describes an aging but no less ardent pair:

> *Your hip replacement mended,*
> *my back pain abated,*
> *our bed that seemed too small*
> *has re-expanded.*

Still another couple in "Watering the New Lawn," by Michael S. Smith, turns gardening into a sensual, erotic pleasure:

> *... This could be our last lawn, we knew,*
> *and aged expertise had taught us to take our sweet*
> *time.*

The overall message contained in the book's last chapter, "Graceful Transformations," was something the poets helped me to understand. I didn't appreciate this concept completely when I began looking for images that celebrate healthy sex. But in their wisdom, in their art, these poets have helped me to see sex as something evolutionary. What higher consciousness are we moving toward with this sexual energy? As our bodies change with age, how do our sexual expressions mature? As we evolve as a couple, what lasting pleasures might we create together?

Sex is momentary, and sex is transcendent. That's the paradox. The most intense physical sharing we experience with another person is gone in a matter of minutes. And yet, it connects us with a larger energy, a life force. Real, authentic intimacy leaves behind an inner glow that warms every aspect of our lives. Sex reminds us of our limitations and our expansiveness as humans. We are alone, and we are together.

Terra Hunter captures this duality beautifully in her poem "Wanting You," as she writes:

> *How is it that our two bodies*
> *made only of flesh and bone*
> *ignite with this fire*
> *yet do not burn?*

How is it that this cannot last
will disappear into the ether
as our bones will turn to dust
and disappear into the earth?

Sexual love is connection, not only with one's partner, but with the elemental beauty of life on earth. Often, when the poets in this collection describe the sensual and transcendental aspects of sex, they use metaphors from nature. A lover's touch becomes the summer heat moving through a canyon. A climax becomes the deepening red colors in a sunset. An embrace becomes the soft inside petals of a flower. The poets reminded me that some of the best images to represent the experience of sexual love are to be found in the natural world. Healthy sexual expression is a natural aspect of life. Tuning into life's natural beauty can stimulate our senses and enhance sexual awareness and enjoyment.

Just as this collection celebrates the natural beauty of every stage of sexual relating, so it can be used to inspire you at all stages of your life. Some poems will sound different to you when you are young, and perhaps just beginning a relationship, than when you are older, and more settled with a partner.

Perhaps you will take time to read these poems together. Love is like a duet, a song you create with your partner. At different times you'll each have passages to sing alone, and passages to sing in harmony with one another. Reading these poems to one another may bring you new inspiration for the unique love song you are creating together. The poets have offered you their gift of words. You and your partner can breathe your own meaning from them.

Healthy sexual relating is a lifelong journey. It's a mystery we unlock through our own experiences. In creating *Passionate Hearts*, I have found some new signposts that help guide the way to a world of healthy sexual loving. As these words dance across the pages and into your lives, may you share the joy that I have found in searching for them.

— W. M.

CHAPTER ONE

tender awakenings

THE TREES THAT CHANGE OUR LIVES

When I was twenty I walked past
The lady I would marry —
Cross-legged on the porch.
She was cracking walnuts
With a hammer, a jar
At her side. I had come
From the store, swinging
A carton of cold beers,
And when I looked she smiled.
And that was all, until
I came back, flushed,
Glowing like a lantern
Against a backdrop
Of silly one-liners —
Cute-face, peaches, baby-lips.

We talked rain, cats,
About rain on cats,
And later went inside
For a sandwich, a glass
Of milk, sweets.
Still later, a month later,
We were going at one
Another on the couch, bed,
In the bathtub

And its backwash of bubbles,
Snapping. So it went,
And how strangely: the walnut
Tree had dropped its hard
Fruit, and they, in turn,
Were dropped into a paper
Bag, a jar, then into
The dough that was twisted
Into bread for the love
Of my mouth, so
It might keep talking.

gary soto

SHARING

outside
        a moon starting up
over a warm summer meadow:
        myriads of fireflies, quietly moving &
                flickering their own type of light
                        to each other
are moving to the slowly increasing magic
        of their closeness
                with this first warm night.

inside
        in the dusk light
of your kitchen
                quietly talking over a table,
and moving closer to each other
                with words,
        & then to the first time   of
                touching hands.
the motion of our hands while talking,
        starting up a beginning
                place of sharing:
a first motion of touching

with a magic possibility
   of keeping the closeness
      of this night,
               inside.

alan yount

SPRING STORM

I stood in the doorway
for the longest time
after you left
looking at the night
    listening to the night
feeling the cold
    against the warmth of my body
feeling your touch
    ripening on my body

It would have been too easy
    to welcome you inside me
succumb to the rhythm
    of waves washing over me

As much as that would be
    it wouldn't be enough

I would never know
    who
    was on the other side
of your skin

johanna rayl

THE RIVER

All the bright day I rode my bike along the river
gold flashing among the dizzy leaves
water clear and rushing over stones
the sound drawing me on.

All day I rode with the wind in my face
till I lost a shoe when I drank at the river
and turned to go home.

It was dusk when I entered the old
house on the hill
and you were glad to see me.

You showed me strings you had tied to a stick.
I watched you dip strings in hot tallow
again and again
while the long tapered bodies grew thick.

Then you lit two of your candles
and there in the flickering shadows we stood
between floors on a landing.
You reached to embrace me as I turned toward you

and gently your lips brushed on my lips
and gently your tongue entered my mouth

finding the way through the dark.

I stood open — river swelling inside me —
rising and falling —
walls breathing for me —

the sound of the river rushed in my ears
my legs were water (I might have fallen
if your arms had not held me).

Finally
you turned with a smile as though it were natural
and walked down the stairs
leaving me filled
with that long trembling.

When I could speak I said, *Let's walk by the river.*
Then I asked, *Will you be loving?*
and laughed at my words.
I meant to say, *"Will you be leaving?"*
and then you laughed too.

A slip of the tongue, you said.
Yes, I said, *a slip of the tongue.*

> *patti tana*

PURPLE IS THE COLOR OF THE LONGING

Purple is the color of the longing
tucked into the folds of pulpy organs
soft and vulnerable.
A finger could pierce like a bullet
this swollen pulse,
an uncaring touch would tear to pieces
the soft fiber of its nest.

Defenseless it hides
in the soft warm dark
    safe and alone
and dreams silently
of the most gentle hands,
hands that part the flesh with trembling care
    inching open the egg,
hands that breathe, warm and moist
    attentive to the quietest heartbeats,
slow, patient hands that touch
    with no shadow of demand,
fingers that explore hinted textures
    radiating wonder and discovery,
bridges delicate enough to join
    one time

under the noise of aching lives
the being of one
with the presence of another.

david steinberg

TANGO'D LOVE

You approach
I stand erect
anticipate extended hand
guides me to the dance floor
slick and satin black reflects
sophisticated bodies glide
forward   backward   heads cocked
hip to hip we promenade
to throbbing music swells   swelling
slow   slow   quick quick   slow
thighs whisper push me pull me
surrender to the pounding beat
accelerates my lower body
undulates back and forth and back
to back vibrations ripple
skin on skin   pulsating
face to face your mouth slides
onto into parted lips
connect the movements quicker
quicker now   you lift me bend
me holding hold me while
the notes explode
Crescendo

j. b. bernstein

With you I begin
to find my body again.
Senses come slowly alive,
sphincters soften,
turtle head rises
    inch by inch
out of shell.

With you I remember
the most basic pattern,
sense the warm pulse,
move closer
    beat by beat.

Pray for safety,
for open arms.
Test twice every reaching.
Hold open the possibility
    so often impossible.
Reach shaking fingertips
out into the blackness
hoping for you to be real,
wanting to trust the touch of you
    and afraid,

find finally
fingers that are not mine
also reaching
also afraid
also beginning to believe
again.

david steinberg

SHE TEACHES HIM TO REACH OUT

Give me your hand. Place it on my bare breast
and take the chance of merging skin with skin.
Your hand will hold the heat when you withdraw it,
leaving a cold, invisible handprint,
change for both of us. Who knows what comes next?
Desire, like any investment, means risk,
for decision is part of sensation
and not the least pleasurable element.

To choose is never a casual act,
nor is love, nor is any handmade gift.
I have unwrapped myself: If you hold back,
your hand will remain empty, a high cost
for no interest. With a single touch,
we balance gain and loss — the feel of choice.

martha elizabeth

I HAVE TOUCHED

your hair
with the palms
of my hands
I have fingered
the strands
around and around

your ears
with my words
I have tickled
with laughter

your neck
with my tongue
with my teeth
with my lips
I have kissed

your thighs
with my thighs
pressing between
ha! I have touched

your feet
your scars

you said you bleed hard
as I traced the soft flesh

your hands
with my hands
your chest
with my chest
and even your heart   yes!
especially your heart

my cheek to your breast
as it rises and falls
my breath in your hair
the wind in the leaves

oh yes these
I have touched.

patti tana

DESIRE

Taking off
my clothes
piece by piece,
I turn to you,
unwrap my body,
feel you trace
its contours
with your fingers.
I am accustomed
to covering,
what I now bare,
watch you waken
and wash me
with your eyes.
I feel the cloth
of your skin,
uncovered,
inviting me in,
feel your breath
warm in my ear.
I lean closer
into you, feel
your blood surge
as you hold me
and I echo

the beat pulling
on us as I wrap
my legs around you
and open as morning
glories do
when the sun
warms them.

connemara wadsworth

FIRST NIGHT

You came into my life
with grace, giving me time
to want all of you. That
first night I couldn't say
whether your passion or
your gentleness moved me
more, the way we took each
other or how we talked
till dawn, our brief sleep a
ceremonial act
in the strangeness of love.

julia h. ackerman

REMEMBERING

Come here, closer, and fold
into the dent of my chest,
the crook of my shoulder.
In the open window the
candle betrays the wind's
summer breath and the
night settles down around us.

Don't move, not now,
let's be still, hold this moment
before we open our bodies,
and tell me, one more time,
how you came to find me.

stephen j. lyons

CHAPTER TWO

passionate pleasures

POEM FOR R.

Above, it's spring, I think,
and kisses bloom over every inch of skin,
each curve and lobe
our rosy lips moisten and shine.

Your body is a new country,
hidden landscape in cotton and chambray
that I want to travel with every vehicle I own:
hands, tongue, slide of silk.

Below, in the heat
and rush of wet, we're learning again
how summer moves through the deep canyons,
stirring grasses and honeying fruit.

How I love your trembling fingers,
given by the gentle ones
who taught you to crave taste and touch.
Under them, I am fully open.

kim ly bui-burton

SNOW CLIMBERS

we touch fingertips
climb feet against feet
toward Sierra peaks
where the air leaps
catch our breath that flies away
with rising birds
and then follow the crevice
where your flesh turns
a long line inward
clear to the small of your back
I move carefully
as a snow climber
near red mountain flowers
while you lead with hips
certain and gentle as a hand

steve wiesinger

TRANSFORMATION

The phoenix is rising:

I see her wings open before me
like a vast awning of light.
I see her feathered petals
begin their ceremony

like tulips opening,
each of their cups
curved upon curve
like the feathers of the great bird.

As if tulips could fly.
As if
the great bird bloomed.

I feel the curves of your fingers,
the ten smooth petals of your hands
as you cup me in front of you,

your lifting chest
curved into the curve of my backbone,
your feathered groin
brushing my two-pillowed rump,
your arms, a circle.

Your fingers circle
like small fledglings,
settle at the edge
of the purple nested flower
with its entrance of folds,

the multi-curved
overlapping, variegated transition . . .

Flesh risen, warm blood,
our bodies
and the bird suspended.

adria klinger

i like my body when it is with your
body. It is so quite new a thing.
Muscles better and nerves more.
i like your body.   i like what it does,
i like its hows.   i like to feel the spine
of your body and its bones,and the trembling
-firm-smooth ness and which i will
again and again and again
kiss,   i like kissing this and that of you,
i like,slowly stroking the,shocking fuzz
of your electric fur, and what-is-it comes
over parting flesh.... And eyes big love-crumbs,

and possibly i like the thrill

of under me you so quite new

e.e. cummings

LATE AFTERNOON

Carry me down into that liquid place again
where we meet without talking, even though
sometimes we're talking, where we laugh
without making a sound, the punchlines
floating off untethered and the corners
of your mouth tilting up like commas
around some beautiful phrase we don't
have to try to remember. Wedge your knee
between my thighs and slip your fingers
into me again, let them be glazed
with human light and lift them to your lips,
let them tell you what they found.
I'll kneel before the sunset of your skin,
its pale tone beginning to blush, evenly,
every cell inspired to red, pushing toward
that ruddiness of purpose, that sigh.
My hands will wrap around the small tendons
of your wrists to hold you here, lowered
over me like clouds before a storm,
the enormous thunder and then the rain.

molly fisk

Half-sleeping,
my body pulls toward yours —
desire a long oar dipping
again and again
in this night's dark rain.

jane hirshfield

MOONBURN

I like my body when you hover over me
in this fragile darkness
It is as if the moon lingers above in sweet,
suspended honey
lighting the empire of flesh
the garden of wild roses
that makes up
us together.

It is the richness of your lips
as they descend towards me;
I open to you like the petals of a rose
when you tell me
of moonburn in whispers with your
eyes;
we tremble
like fading galaxies wrapped in silk,
like wind in leaves under
a fading moon.

laura h. kennedy

MORNING LOVE SONG

I am filled with love like a melon
with seeds, I am ripe and dripping sweet juices.
If you knock gently on my belly
it will thrum ripe, ripe.

It is high green summer with the strawberries
just ending and the blueberries coloring,
with the roses tumbling like fat Persian
kittens, the gold horns of the squash blowing.

The day after a storm the leaves gleam.
The world is clear as a just washed picture window.
The air whips its fine silk through the hands.
Every last bird has an idea to insist on.

I am trying to work and instead
I drip love for you like a honeycomb.
I am devoid of fantasies clean as rainwater
waiting to flow all over your skin.

marge piercy

fortunately the skins
peel back to let
us in
feelings of pulp moving
under the mouth who finds
how sweet to be
how blonde your
hips fit

I kiss your
ears your blood
bangs into my
love my life
beats
sing it

fortunately the skins shout
tambourine speeches
we understand
brush of your hair in
my ears who find your
belly a white drum thumping
snare to come upon how
blonde you are

I suck your
lips your teeth
bite into my
life my red love
take it

judy grahn

MARVELOUS BEAST

suspended from
    your animal form
        arms and legs circling
    bodies touching
            then glancing away

the tease of your nearness
    and parting excites me
        and now I am striding
    at ease with your bigness
my pleasure spreading
           in widening spheres

and now we are moving
    faster and faster
        though still unhurried
    knowing this lasts
knowing how far
        we can ride

and now I am
    urging you enter
        the quickening center
    everything in me
           shaped to an O

patti tana

UNTITLED I

I am in the most exquisite distress
astride you now,
sweating
feeling an impetuous volcano
strain at its peak
inside
wanting to explode
my sweetest self
all over you.

laura h. kennedy

LOVERS' DUET

What began as an urge to satisfy
something primal in me,
became a desire to unite deeply
with you.

I rose in love to your touch.
I lost myself in the fullness of your kiss,
the silky glide of your arms,
the strong harbor of your thighs,
the heat of your body
inside mine.

I opened to you
as you opened to me,
parting barriers unfelt until
we pressed freely beyond their sphere.

You moved with love,
holding me firmly,
giving me pleasure,
carefully stroking me fuller, harder,
more vulnerable.

Beyond the rattle of the clock
and the confines of the room.
Beyond cumbersome egos
and the constant pressure of earthly concerns.

Into an ancient rhythmical dance,
a duet of quickening passions,
breathless friction,
breathful sighs.
Your joy beckoned mine,
and mine yours.

Steadily rocking,
rolling through cannonball bursts
and delicate pulsations.
We came cheek to cheek,
sharing a sweet throaty song
of *I Love Yous*.

wendy lee

LEARNING TO LAUGH

At first I laughed to hide my nervousness,
my hand closed over my mouth
to silence that titter,
an uncertain sound
I didn't, couldn't control.

Breasts exposed, thighs
uncovered, I'd been found out,
caught, held up under daylight
for inspection, my chest
rising and falling with each

sharp intake of breath.
Then I learned to melt
into your hands, sliding
into pleasure when your lips
met mine, labia parted

for your tongue, mouth
open as I gasped, nerves
signaling bliss. I pulled
you closer in, reveled
in joy so profound

that I couldn't help laughing
a full-bodied laugh that rang
through the dormant building,
waking the sleeping, the drunk.
I laughed so low, so deep,

that I couldn't believe such a sound
could come from my naked body,
the same flesh that once
could only titter in shame.
What finally did it? Your hands,

those fingers, that didn't stop
touching every sexual place:
nape of the neck, bare lower
back, undersides of breasts.
Determined, those hands

set loose a woman not sated
with quick meeting, mating,
worked corners, crevices —
until that laugh came bubbling
out of me, sudden rapture

I didn't deny, a sound that would never
be furtive again, proud and loud instead,
so loud that neighbors must wonder
what it is you're giving me,
their ears burning when they hear

the laughs that just keep
coming, rising out of me
to stop traffic on the boulevard,
drivers slowing to listen
to the most joy they've ever heard.

allison joseph

AUBADE

The geese flew by as you entered me,
Crying in joy at coming home again
To the river.

The sounds of the geese rose
As our throats swelled with
Waves of pleasure.

And as the gray wings sounded
In the sky, gray light
Filled the room

Where our bodies lay entwined
On the shores
Of dawn.

"Imagine," you said, rolling away,
"A lifetime. A lifetime
Of Sunday mornings."

Then I saw our love spread out
Onto a sea of Sundays, ringed by
Beaches of weekday cares.

We heard the geese land on the river,
Sinking into the green waves as
We turned to each other,
Opened our hearts' wings, and
Flew into the morning.

kate c. richardson

Good God, what a night that was,
The bed was so soft, and how we clung,
Burning together, lying this way and that,
Our uncontrollable passions
Flowing through our mouths.
If I could only die that way,
I'd say goodbye to the business of living.

petronius arbiter
[translated from the Greek by *kenneth rexroth*]

THE MORNING AFTER

The morning after
I turn lazily in bed
snuggling under covers
that so recently enveloped you.

I seem to take forever
to open my eyes,
not wanting to see the empty place
you left behind.

I bury my nose
in pillows and linen
to catch a lingering scent of you...

I pull back the sheets
and smile tenderly at all the hair
you left... the dark curly evidence
scattered everywhere.

The morning after
I lose myself in the night before
hugging myself, caressing me —
though not as well as you do,
dreaming still, of nights to come.

johari m. rashad

LOVE POEM

olfactory paradise
> scent of musk and sweat
>> mingling on fingers and thighs

emerald ferns
> wet with morning
smell of loam
> rich moist earth
salty spray
> glistening lips

amber drenched tongues of flame
> licking the senses

electric pulse
> flashing indigo and violet
night storm singing
> silver edged midnight
>> scented with thunder.

e. k. caldwell

AN AUBADE

As she is showering, I wake to see
A shine of earrings on the bedside stand,
A single yellow sheet which, over me,
Has folds as intricate as drapery
In paintings from some fine old master's hand.

The pillow which, in dozing, I embraced
Retains the salty sweetness of her skin;
I sense her smooth back, buttocks, belly, waist,
The leggy warmth which spread and gently laced
Around my legs and loins, and drew me in.

I stretch and curl about a bit and hear her
Singing among the water's hiss and race.
Gradually the early light makes clearer
The perfume bottles by the dresser's mirror,
The silver flashlight, standing on its face,

Which shares the corner of the dresser with
An ivy spilling tendrils from a cup.
And so content am I, I can forgive
Pleasure for being brief and fugitive.
I'll stretch some more, but postpone getting up

Until she finishes her shower and dries
(Now this and now that foot placed on a chair)
Her fineboned ankles, and her calves and thighs,
The pink full nipples of her breasts, and ties
Her towel up, turban-style, about her hair.

timothy steele

ALONE IN YOUR HOUSE

I walk naked and
dripping to the kitchen,

the floor sticky,
rubbing myself

with your damp towel.
When I go out on the porch

two fawns get up
from the grass.

We have surprised each other;
their soft black noses

swing away from my breasts,
quivering.

I remember you nuzzling me,
raising my hips,

my cheek against the mattress buttons.
The little deer

have been at the berries,
nibbling stems. The doe eases out

from the bushes,
juice streaking her flanks.

They follow her away down the hill
and the wet

flattened grass
slowly rises behind them.

kim addonizio

WOMAN BATHING

Naches River. Just below the falls.
Twenty miles from any town. A day
of dense sunlight
heavy with odors of love.
How long have we?
Already your body, sharpness of Picasso,
is drying in this highland air.
I towel down your back, your hips,
with my undershirt.
Time is a mountain lion.
We laugh at nothing,
and as I touch your breasts
even the ground-
               squirrels
are dazzled.

raymond carver

LAST GODS

She sits naked on a rock
a few yards out in the water.
He stands on the shore,
also naked, picking blueberries.
She calls. He turns. She opens
her legs showing him her great beauty,
and smiles, a bow of lips
seeming to tie together
the ends of the earth.
Splashing her image
to pieces, he wades out
and stands before her, sunk
to the anklebones in leaf-mush
and bottom-slime — the intimacy
of the visible world. He puts
a berry in its shirt
of mist into her mouth.
She swallows it. He puts in another.
She swallows it. Over the lake
two swallows whim, juke, jink,
and when one snatches
an insect they both whirl up
and exult. He is swollen
not with ichor but with blood.
She takes him and sucks him

more swollen. He kneels, opens
the dark, vertical smile
linking heaven with the underearth
and licks her smoothest flesh more smooth.
On top of the rock they join.
Somewhere a frog moans, a crow screams.
The hair of their bodies
startles up. They cry
in the tongue of the last gods,
who refused to go,
chose death, and shuddered
in joy and shattered in pieces,
bequeathing their cries
into the human mouth. Now in the lake
two faces float, looking up
at a great maternal pine whose branches
open out in all directions
explaining everything.

galway kinnell

THE IMAGE WAS OF ME FLOWING THROUGH YOU

The image was of me flowing through you
everywhere,
all the membranes gone transparent,
the holding released
and so a washing.
I felt me pouring, and you.

You knew then all that I knew,
arms and legs circling,
the core enclosed,
the two/one of us
balanced and still.

Oh the welcome, the ease,
the walls saturated,
slithering into soft mounds.

We breathed,
we drank,
taking care not to tear the lace.

david steinberg

LOOK AT ME

you answered, when I held you
with my arms and sex,
when I said you could come, when
I asked what you wanted.
Look at me.

The soft of your belly tightened,
pushing curve against sway,
my tongue pressing
the gray whorls of hair
hiding your thick and beating heart,

I opened my eyes to you
intent, warm
blue-eyed familiar
holding tightly to my arms;
you were almost there.

Your body lifted mine
with each rising breath,
keening, gasping
and when you came
I looked deep

in the wet and darkening irises,
caught the sweet of your sperm
between my legs,
met your fierce
and shining gaze,

— look at me —
you whispered and I did.
I did.

kim ly bui-burton

MY GOD, WHY ARE YOU CRYING?

When someone cries, after making love spills
a pail of tears inside, it is the ache
of years, all the early years' emptiness
hollowed into a pail-like form which fills
with feeling now felt aloud, that resounds.

Why would an orgasm make someone weep?
Why, for being loved now when one had not been.
The anger tendered into tears astounds
the lover with fear to have struck so deep.

molly peacock

MIDNIGHT

After making love
beneath the wings of the ceiling fan,
we will rappel,
make our unnatural descent,
step off the sheer cliff of waketime.

Soon we will let go
of the muslin drapes and high, white walls
and you will slip
into rhythmic breathing, your limbs
trembling down the length of sleep.

You will use your arms
to control the downward slide; your knees
wedged inside mine,
your hand bracing my hip, your scent
enclosing me in this cocoon.

And breath after breath,
we will let the reliable cues
swallow us down
like gravity, until we fall
untied in our naked safety.

alison kolodinsky

SEX HAS A WAY

Sex has a way of softening limbs,
oiling joints and melding hearts.

We burrow in closer
wrapping arms and legs over and under each other.

Earthy blanket of sleep covers us
two bodies releasing one breath.

Finding home,
coiled and tucked in each other's sweat.

wendy lee

DESIRE

We leave the bed where your fingers
are a wide surprise, where your tongue
tells me slow stories. I watch you,
in the daylight, bring your hand
to your face, to your mouth. I tuck
pieces of myself behind
in the tangle of our bodies.
We make our way onto buses,
we pass the old women who sit
rocking and tapping their feet,
we blow our noses, clear our throats.
It's just life picking us up,
moving us from one place to
the next. We fumble for our keys,
tie our shoes, greet people we
care nothing for greeting. But
today, when you reach into your
pocket, you'll find the curve of my
neck, you'll brush away my hair
from your cheek. I'll slip inside
your shirt, lie flat against your chest.
Your hands will catch themselves
reaching. And the scent of me, the
scent you long for, will draw you home.

kim ports

ALL DAY AT WORK

All day at work
I carry the scent of you.
I touch my fingers to my lips.
I remember this morning
how your lips parted
as though there was some secret
you had been holding,
were finally ready to share.

The telephone rings.
I press my ear to the receiver,
just as I laid it last night
into the place between your breasts.
Your heart beats loudly;
I must ask the woman who has called
to repeat what she is saying.
I keep trying to distinguish her words
from the rhythm I have memorized in sleep.

I type letters in the afternoon.
I put the date at the top of each clean page.
Your thighs are nearly this white
and just as smooth.

When I am finished
I run my finger along the crease
as though even this fold
might arouse to my touch.

I drive home the long way.
The ocean is the color of your eyes.
There is a little boat off in the distance,
the faint image of a person aboard.
I am looking into your dark centers
where I see myself reflected,
standing close to the edge,
as though I might
at any moment
take in my breath and dive down.

deborah abbott

GIVING THANKS

You would not believe it; I sat
at the table with my family,
with my father saying grace, then
solemnly passing the bowls of
corn, of beans, the heavy
platter of turkey and dressing.
I filled my plate and lifted
my fork to my mouth,
but no matter what I put in,
it wasn't what I tasted,
not the creamed potatoes,
not the smooth brown crust
of bread. It was you my mouth
remembered, the familiar musk
of your sex, its smooth heat,
its quick fullness. My mind was
a reel flashing pictures inside
my skull, and there was no detail
missing. I sat like a drunk
trying to act sober. I chewed
and swallowed while in my thoughts
I knelt; I gave thanks for you.

anne k . smith

WANTING YOU

Driving north out of town today
through cornfields
and newly plowed patches of earth
looking at the dark rich soil
I wanted you,
wanted you to press yourself into me
press me into the open field
until my curves
become the contours of the ground beneath us.

Your arms tight around me
your mouth tender
your tongue insistent
on my lips skin neck breasts
your fingers delicate
along my back
like the wind across the top of the grass.

I split open
like the earth ripped apart in a quake
a deep valley suddenly empty
longing to be filled
as if you entering me would bring us both
into the dark mystery of the earth herself.

How is it that our two bodies
made only of flesh and bone
ignite with this fire
yet do not burn?

How is it that this cannot last
will disappear into the ether
as our bones will turn to dust
and disappear into the earth?

terra hunter

PRIVACY

Finally
the only one I want
    to caress is you

You watch the changing
light across the sky
    I watch your eyes

     olga broumas

CHAPTER THREE

varied dances

IMPLICATIONS OF ONE PLUS ONE

Sometimes we collide, tectonic plates merging,
continents shoving, crumpling down into the molten
veins of fire deep in the earth and raising
tons of rock into jagged crests of Sierra.

Sometimes your hands drift on me, milkweed's
airy silk, wingtip's feathery caresses,
our lips grazing, a drift of desires gathering
like fog over warm water, thickening to rain.

Sometimes we go to it heartily, digging,
burrowing, grunting, tossing up covers
like loose earth, nosing into the other's
flesh with hot nozzles and wallowing there.

Sometimes we are kids making out, silly
in the quilt, tickling the xylophone spine,
blowing wet jokes, loud as a whole
slumber party bouncing till the bed breaks.

I go round and round you sometimes, scouting,
blundering, seeking a way in, the high boxwood
maze I penetrate running lungs bursting
toward the fountain of green fire at the heart.

Sometimes you open wide as cathedral doors
and yank me inside. Sometimes you slither
into me like a snake into its burrow.
Sometimes you march in with a brass band.

Ten years of fitting our bodies together
and still they sing wild songs in new keys.
It is more and less than love: timing,
chemistry, magic and will and luck.

One plus one equal one, unknowable except
in the moment, not convertible into words,
not explicable or philosophically interesting.
But it is. And it is. And it is. Amen.

marge piercy

WITH THANKS TO EDDIE SHAW

Late Friday
we watched Eddie blow the blues
through his sax,
make love to the brass piece
that fell between his thighs
like a stallion's money.
Eddie sweated his shirt black
while we moved across the floor
smooth as Irish whiskey,
eyes and belt buckles locked into each other.
When Eddie moaned "The Thrill is Gone,"
we knew he wasn't singing for us.
We gave the floor to the blues
when Eddie snaked through the crowd
blowin' that sax like it was a last kiss.
Before he left he shook my hand and said,
"Thank you for listening."
"Man, Eddie," I said, "the thanks are all mine."
We went home to finish what we
started on the dance floor.
I felt the sax slip between my thighs,
drip gold notes, not blue.

janet lowe

FLIGHT FROM THE MARRIAGE BED

one evening, we entered our room with . . .

a kiss, a smile, and
i sit as he strips quickly, gracefully.
in silhouette and shadow,
he is a long-bodied bird, standing,
arms moving like wings.
opening, closing,
he removes my shirt, adds kisses
to tempt as he coaxes fledgling flight.
breast skin freed from cover, i grow alert at the sight,
the sense of his hovering form. his lips peck my shoulder.
i fall back on the bed, lift hips for pants peeling, and ascend
as he lowers his body to nest upon mine. we become

. . . two birds soaring who share
the clouds, clear winds aloft,
the swaying treetops
as easily as breathing.

lisa m. carbone

HER BACK TO ME

I watch her silhouette
in the green glow
of alarm clock light,
imagine the lace of freckles
draped across her back,
inhale the tumble of hair,
cataracting over shoulders.
I reach around,
feel her fullness,
slowly enter.
She molds to me
gentler than any cloud
has ever drifted
across a starlit sky,
and I am a prayer,
a ghost, a vapor,
nebulous as the night.

ed stever

THE PURR

As you stand still in the hall thinking what
to do next and I approach you from behind,
I think behind must be best: your naked
rump scalloped beneath the plumb

line of your spine's furred tree. But
as I catch the concentration in the kind
angling of your head toward the cats and tread
cat-like myself behind you, your scrotum

hung like an oriole's nest, I cut
beneath your outstretched arm and find
I'm hungry for your face instead,
hungry for my future. The mysterious thrum

that science can't yet explain awakes a hum
in me, the sound something numb come alive makes.

molly peacock

MUSIC

As I lie next to you
I am your violin
all smooth curves
waiting to be played upon

as you lie next to me
you are my bow
straight and thin
rigidly poised
in expectation

slowly you fine-tune my body
listening for the different sounds
our music makes
as your bow glides
over my body

at first tentatively
testing the chords
then gently
plucking at the strings

until the soft humming
becomes a duet
then a string ensemble
some brass joins in
finally the full orchestra
explodes in a symphony
of cymbals and drums

the applause is silent

natasha josefowitz

WET BODIES

blood surges in my temples
like intimate tributaries

the moment stands still like a
series of motionless somersaults

the night is consecrated
inundated by glistening grandeur
if I were a mosquito I would
spend my time taking little bites

what the hell I'll do it anyway

you lie in perfect languidness
full of pulse and oily scent
at the mouth of your delta
where everything is pure salt

when you open your thighs
it is the parting of clouds
sparks flying from the hearth
the tides awash over soft fur
the purple conch the huge
wings unfolding the inward explosion
of breath quicksilver in the shape

of hearts that familiar intoxicating
slick reptilian splendor where I shed
skin after skin and crawl like the
consummate cave dweller inside of you

franz douskey

IN BED THIS MORNING

In bed this morning

you tucked into the cove of my belly

our feet slipping past each other like fish

I reached out to embrace

the flat rock of your back

and carved out our names

with my tongue

teresa blagg

TOUCHING YOU UNDER WATER

I want to find your texture under water
in the darkest night, with my hands
open, like the blind who can move
on a current of breath and odor.
It's their strange luck to have this touch:
leaf to branch, water to shore,
hand to cheek. To know
the difference between tears and rain;
morning's dampness. In the black
pools, where the moon rests,
and rainbows rise
I want to lift you above the wetness
and watch stars spark over
your shoulders and feel the
brush of air as you take flight.

stephen j. lyons

Drunk as drunk on turpentine
From your open kisses,
Your wet body wedged
Between my wet body and the strake
Of our boat that is made out of flowers,
Feasted, we guide it — our fingers
Like tallows adorned with yellow metal —
Over the sky's hot rim,
The day's last breath in our sails.

Pinned by the sun between solstice
And equinox, drowsy and tangled together
We drifted for months and woke
With the bitter taste of land on our lips,
Eyelids all sticky, and we longed for lime
And the sound of a rope
Lowering a bucket down its well. Then,
We came by night to the Fortunate Isles,
And lay like fish
Under the net of our kisses.

> *pablo neruda*
> [translated from Spanish by *christopher logue*]

LOVING ALONG WESTERN RIVERS
— *for jan*

Pull the car off here
in the tall rushes
of mock orange and wild rose.
Deep along riverbanks of late spring
runoff there is one spot of blue sky,
one chance between storms to touch
and we're hungry for skin.

Set up the hot tent near the shore
so the water moves beneath us
as you move beneath me.
Somewhere distant voices of rafters
reach us, like sound on a shelf.
Inside, you hold me back, make me wait,
tell me I'm slippery and wipe me down,
with a blue towel moving
your hips the entire time.

There are purple river rocks,
older than this brief time
we've been given to do this,
to merge at the confluence,
to boil in the white glare.
Open mouth tasting salt.

Sweat and saliva.
Raising of hips, belly to belly,
there's no turning back,
we want each other
and nothing will stop us
from loving, along Western rivers.

stephen j. lyons

COMPLICATED SHADOWS

To hawks we're a woodland insect,
four legs above and four below, twitching
on the ground as if a flash-tongued sun
sought to flicker through us to the spot we've claimed.

Each small move we make is shading for one,
quick burning for the other — our bodies
become one another's clothing tugged off,
wrapped on, stripped away again in glowing haste.

The question of shadows gains depth
when our stomachs press close
to leave no space from skin to skin,
sealing a damp plane between us,
a pressure of pure darkness
we feel but cannot see:
light needs at least a chance to be absent —
no shadows in locked closets,
behind closed lids, within the heart's chambers.

We are weaving and folding, we
know this soil is a great compost heap,
we are making and unmaking
light — forcing the aging hot sun to run.

stephen corey

THE MUSIC LIKE WATER

How, on a summer night,
the mysterious few bird notes rise
and break against the dark and stop,
and that music continues, afterward, for a long time;
how you move in me until silence itself is moving
precisely as those few notes,
how they do not stop, the music like water
finding its way;
how what we begin we only think is ours,
how quickly it passes from reach,
some other life throating the air
until it is utterly lovely and changed;
how I am changed by you and change you,
how we willingly hollow our throats for the song,
how the music chains us, but the song —
on a summer night, how it breaks and stops,
how we falter and still the notes rise, beyond us,
how they complete themselves in the silence
and silence completes us, simple as those few notes
that answer the dark on a summer night and fall still.

jane hirshfield

MY LOVE IS LIKE A LILY

but what flowers is not his face —
roughly bearded, creased
and lined by the sun.
The stem of his body
unfolds into smoothness,
wrapping the good bones and veins
for my touch.
Where the rivers fork,
he grows a field of grassy
darkness. I follow his legs,
like the deep roots
of mandrake, below ground
where his feet stir the dark
under covers. Tracing them back,
I taste him
salty, bitter,
ready for planting.
With my warm hands,
I hold the heavy bulb
between our legs,
embracing that other stem,
the smooth-budded one.

We garden in darkness,
burying the stalk of his flowering
deep into me.
This is our season:
the night-blooming one.

kim ly bui-burton

LULLABY

Big as a down duvet the night
pulls the close Canadian sky
over the naked earth. Here we lie
gossiping in a circle of light

under our own big comforter,
buried nude as bulbs. I slide south
to grow your hyacinth in my mouth.
Far above, the constellations blur

on the comforter that real sky
is to real earth. Stars make a pattern
above; down here our pattern is fireflies
on flannel around us. Night turns

to surround the planet. Earth settles
real hyacinths in place. You yield,
turning like night's face to settle
on me, chest on breasts, your field.

molly peacock

THE BLOSSOM

When we love, clouds
of early spring fly over,
neither snow nor rain.
A joy whose name
waits to be spoken
hides in the new moon.
At the edge of the bed,
you tighten your legs
on my waist. How many
centuries have we
done this thing?
What was sleeping
between our thighs hears
the flute sound
that persuaded the tulip
to throw open the bulb's
bronze door. Our most
sheltered bud,
when it meets another,
falls into a wild desire
to unfold itself and
become a blossom —

all children, reckless,
ride into this world
on the promise
of that burning blossom.

thomas r. smith

NEW MOTHER

A week after our child was born,
you cornered me in the spare room
and we sank down on the bed.
You kissed me and kissed me, my milk undid its
burning slip-knot through my nipples,
soaking my shirt. All week I had smelled of milk,
fresh milk, sour. I began to throb:
my sex had been torn easily as cloth by the
crown of her head, I'd been cut with a knife and
sewn, the stitches pulling at my skin —
and the first time you're broken, you don't know
you'll be healed again, better than before.
I lay in fear and blood and milk
while you kissed and kissed me, your lips hot and swollen
as a teen-age boy's, your sex dry and big,
all of you so tender, you hung over me,
over the nest of stitches, over the
splitting and tearing, with the patience of someone who
finds a wounded animal in the woods
and stays with it, not leaving its side
until it is whole, until it can run again.

sharon olds

MILKFLOWERS

It is first that angle at which you sleep,
canted, neither on your back nor your side
but in between. The baby, fallen asleep at last,
must let go his latch, and your nipple
gummed these months to impossible softness
slowly oozes one sweet delinquent drop.

But sweet as it is, I don't take it,
because it is not this richness I crave
but its ghost, glimmering silver in the light of candles,
dried by my breath softly blowing . . .

Thus, when the baby is tucked in his cradle,
I lick my lips and kiss your milk-anointed breasts
until my mouth is glazed with the purest sugar,
then knead from each nipple one additional drop to dry,
and begin, all down the trellis of bones,
to paint your skin with invisible roses.

robert wrigley

BALANCE

Next summer she'll be too old for naps,
but this July, with the right story
and patience, you can still
settle her down in our bed
in the wide berth of a weekend afternoon.

And that's why making love now
we're in her small room. Where you shift
on top. Where we coax and quicken
and your right hand,
braced against the wall,
inches up cool plaster.

Wind pushes in again and again,
always leaving slack the blind
to knock against the sash.

Yet, we feel no breeze through the window —
as if the blind's tugged inward
to balance a recurring loss of pressure
elsewhere in the house.

james harris

AFTER MAKING LOVE WE HEAR FOOTSTEPS

For I can snore like a bullhorn
or play loud music
or sit up talking with any reasonably sober Irishman
and Fergus will only sink deeper
into his dreamless sleep, which goes by all in one flash,
but let there be that heavy breathing
or a stifled come-cry anywhere in the house
and he will wrench himself awake
and make for it on the run — as now, we lie together,
after making love, quiet, touching along the length
    of our bodies,
familiar touch of the long-married,
and he appears — in his baseball pajamas, it happens,
the neck opening so small he has to screw them on —
and flops down between us and hugs us and snuggles
    himself to sleep,
his face gleaming with satisfaction at being this very child.

In the half darkness we look at each other
and smile
and touch arms across this little, startlingly muscled body —
this one whom habit of memory propels to the ground
    of his making,
sleeper only the mortal sounds can sing awake,
this blessing love gives again into our arms.

    galway kinnell

ANNIVERSARY

This is not first love.
In the next rooms our two children
breathe the air of dreams,
and down the street a house
is being robbed,
and the selectmen are up late
trying to cut the budget.
You and I hold one another
between these worlds, these walls,
these sheets and arms
until we become
first lovers
again.

gary metras

DESCANT

Outside our bedroom window
in the dark of a spring
rainy midnight
a lone bird warbled
its varied love song
as if it knew what
we were doing
with our windows open.
It trilled on for an hour
in the middle of that night
singing descant
to my heart's melody.

jane mayes

DOG DAYS AND DELTA NIGHTS

Standing knee-deep in Oak Creek
while snakes slither like flexible
tubing in the delicate moonlight,
everything moves slowly to cool off.
Too hot to even speak, while a persimmon
leaf takes the shape of water and floats by.

Heat lightning in the eastern sky gives
sycamores eerie shadows, as birds wake
now and then, unprotected and complaining,
while you stand naked, beautiful,
hair shining like a pitchfork of summer hay.

I look at the stars,
then at your nipples, glistening, as water
retreats over your skin. You know
my mind. You shake your mane. You
move toward slippery rocks and
the roar of riprap. Up, up, out
of water, the stream racing down your
skin, leaving your body hair smooth.

Up on a flat, mossy rock, you do a
little dance with your hips. You open
your legs a little, then open your lips.
This is sinful all right. Some gospel
fire might find us, but there are certain
pleasures that can't be neglected,

so, call me crawling kingsnake
with a mojo moan, as I move out
of water, rising and filling with blood.

In a moment I am flung inside,
dazzled and dizzy, at times hanging
upside down, waiting for the right
time while you buck and bite.

Shuddering deep, you throw back
a moan across thickets, broken
branches, down by the deer crossing;
so deep, we hunt with our mouths
and forget who we are.

Call it temporary sanity. Great
horse, great mare,
the shadows dissolve, everything
aquiver, our tongues feeling out
the mother language in primitive dance,
hunkering in our wild, wet hides.

Later, we get dressed in cool, orange
light. Get back home before morning
chores, before the kids wake up
so breakfast is ready, and when we
touch they think we just got up,
your eyes speaking for you, and
I let my silence speak for me.

franz douskey

IT ARRIVES SUDDENLY AND CARRIES US OFF AS USUAL

Sometimes in early June I am standing
under the just unpacked green of the oak
when a hot bearish paw suddenly flattens the air:
a warm front marches in palpable as
a shove, a sudden fanfare from the brass.

I am putting dishes away in the cupboard.
You are screwing a bulb into the fixture:
is it the verb, the analogy, the mischievous
child of the limbic brain fitting shards together?
We both think of sex as if a presence

had entered the room, a scent of salt
and hot feathers, a musky tickle
along the spine like arpeggios
galloping down the scale to the bass
that resonates from skull to soles.

The body that has been functioning,
a tidy machine, retracts its armor
of inattention and the skin shimmers
with mouths of light crying let me take
you in, I must be laved in touch.

Now, now. Five minutes later
we are upstairs, the phone out of the wall,
doors locked, clothes tossed like casualties
through three rooms. We are efficient
in our hunger, neat as a sharp-shin stooping.

Half an hour after that we are back,
me at the cupboard, you on the ladder
our clothes rumpled, reeking of secretions
and satisfaction, dazed as if carried
to a height and dropped straight down.

marge piercy

THE THIEF

What is it when your man sits on the floor
in sweatpants, his latest project
set out in front of him like a small world, maps
and photographs, diagrams and plans, everything
he hopes to build, invent or create,
and you believe in him as you always have,
even after the failures, even more now
as you set your coffee down
and move toward him, to where he sits
oblivious of you, concentrating
in a square of sun —
you step over the rulers and blue graph-paper
to squat behind him, and he barely notices,
though you're still in your robe
which falls open a little as you reach
around his chest, feel for the pink
wheel of each nipple, the slow beat
of his heart, your ear pressed to his back
to listen — and you are torn,
not wanting to interrupt his work
but unable to keep your fingers
from dipping into the ditch in his pants,
torn again with tenderness
for the way his flesh grows unwillingly
toward your curved palm, toward the light,

as if you had planted it, this sweet root,
your mouth already an echo of its shape —
you slip your tongue into his ear
and he hears you, calling him away
from his work, the angled lines of his thoughts,
into the shapeless place you are bound
to take him, over bridges of bone, beyond
borders of skin, climbing over him
into the world of the body, its labyrinth
of ladders and stairs — and you love him
like the first time you loved him,
with equal measures of expectancy
and fear and awe, taking him with you
into the soft geometry of the flesh, the earth
before its sidewalks and cities,
its glistening spires,
stealing him back from the world he loves
into this other world he cannot build without you.

dorianne laux

DOLCE

Afterwards, in the shower
part of you escapes me
part of you always runs away
and I cover the loss.

My lipstick glides competently
over the curve that could smile
over the color of passion
that matches the rose still blooming
in my nipples. I ignore the perfume

remembered scent of you
I cannot wash away
memory of our touching
in my fingertips, my flesh
which cringes against
the roughness of clothes.

I brush my hair up
over my ears, wanting to hear
the song beneath your long silences
remaining deaf until you touch me again
    not hello-wife
    I need mother, or
    sexy feelie Playboy grabbie

but who you are
connecting with who I am
making me tremble
like a stroked violin
the pulled bow teasing, pleading
until the moving music
wafts from us   vibrato
vibrato   pizzicato
dolce   dolce   dolce.

kennette wilkes

NO

I will not speak
when words stick in my throat like bricks,
when all words say *love me*
love me as I love you.

I will not speak
when I am feeling like a wall of bricks
that runs along the bottom of a hill
where water seeps.

Touching the wall
moss springs green and soft and moist
and silent as the forest after rain
before birds learned to sing.

No, I will not speak
when I would rather touch.

patti tana

Slowly, slowly
we grow together,
skin across the wound
of our separateness.

david steinberg

THUNDER STORM

Wind rocks our tent. The storm
staggers among the trees.
High in the cave of night
the two Bears roll over, thunder
rumbles down. Why
did we quarrel? We curl up,
my knees in the hollows of yours,
my hand on your mound. Love,
I kiss your neck and you laugh.
Against my thighs I feel
your flesh push and give.
Late at night we listen
to the rain, falling asleep.

Our tent, drenched, gleaming,
leans in that green hush
before morning. How long
since we heard the rain
stop? Quiet, still drowsy,
we stroke each other. *Whik-*
whik, whik-whik. What's that?
We sit up, unzip the flap —
In the dripping light the trees
breathe birds into the sky.

george keithley

LITTLE INVITATION IN A HUSHED VOICE

Even birds help
each other. Come
close. Closer.
Help me
      kiss you.

tess gallagher

CHAPTER FOUR

deeper intimacies

THE MYSTERY

Your eyes drink of me,
    Love makes them shine,
Your eyes that lean
    So close to mine.

We have long been lovers,
    We know the range
Of each other's moods
    And how they change;

But when we look
    At each other so
Then we feel
    How little we know;

The spirit eludes us,
    Timid and free —
Can I ever know you
    Or you know me?

sara teasdale

TO DRINK

I want to gather your darkness
in my hands, to cup it like water
and drink.
I want this in the same way
as I want to touch your cheek —
it is the same —
the way a moth will come
to the bedroom window in late September,
beating and beating its wings against cold glass;
the way a horse will lower
its long head to water, and drink,
and pause to lift its head and look,
and drink again,
taking everything in with the water,
everything.

jane hirshfield

RED RIVER

It's true, I could hold you
after a night of laughing, say,
watching Montgomery Clift
and John Wayne trail their cattle
through Mexico, southern Texas.
And when the movie's over
and the rinsed dishes are shining
in the drainer like the faces of good children,
the wine bottle set by the back door,
glowing faintly green in the dark,
nighthawks will scatter their sharp cries
into the streetlamp's yellow halo
and the moon will begin her steady
descent, and you'll find your way somehow
inside me, tonguing my breasts, gently
closing my eyelids with the calloused tips
of your fingers, bending me
backward over the sofa's ready arm,
but it's not enough, I want you
closer. I want you to pull me inside you,
open your warm skin like a raccoon coat
and wrap it around me, I want to inhabit
the tightening muscles, curl up in your dense,
well-marrowed bones, feel what you touch,
roll the gold vowels of my own name

around in your mouth before they're spoken,
our blood drifting down through the same
dark river, mingled together. I don't know
which is worse: coming, or watching you come.

molly fisk

THE RETURN

When I open my legs to let you seek,
seek inside me, seeking more, I think
"What are you looking for?" and feel it will
be hid from me, whatever it is, still
or rapidly moving beyond my frequency.
Then I declare you a mystery
and stop myself from moving and hold still
until you can find your orgasm. Peak
is partly what you look for, and the brink
you love to come to and return to must
be part of it, too, thrust, build, the trust
that brings me, surprised, to a brink of my own . . .
I must be blind to something of my own
you recognize and look for. A diamond
speaks in a way through its beams, though it's dumb
to the brilliance it reflects. A gem at the back
of the cave must tell you, "Yes, you can go back."

molly peacock

KEYS

Often, I wonder, who is this stranger
come into the season of my unfolding
gently reaching toward me
with a silently mouthed hello.

I've traced the contours of your body with my fingers
I know your taste and the smell of you.
And when we make love, I feel your language
and watch the layers of your defenses become thinner.
Sometimes so fragile that I could break through them
completely
With a word
Or just the slight pressure of my kiss.

I choose not to.
My wish is not to conquer, but to share.
The key to you remains always with you.
Any door you open
I shall gladly walk through.
As for myself . . .
my locks grow weaker.

barbara j. garshman

A NEED FOR ARMOR

polished now
from love's steady
partnership

you feel your way
fluidly
toward warm familiar

destinations
inner pools
unaware

you too
have outgrown
the need for armor

eileen stratidakis

He kneels on the rumpled bed
stroking color on my long toes,
seen, not felt, while my legs and feet
twitch with the strain
of self-imposed restraint.
His intentness on this new task
jabs my jaded heart.

He blows on the nails to dry them,
cradles the other foot and paints slowly.
I lie filled with the wait for the next thing,
the path he will kiss on my legs.

Nothing will happen to wake
the old ghosts in their graves;
their finger bones will not twitch
with memories of touching younger me.
These cries will be wild and joyous.

gail morse

WAKING UP TWICE

Blue-black of a winter morning.
Six o'clock. Between ghosts of houses
the lighter horizontal of the street.
We make an attempt at waking, open
our eyes, our covers, our untried hopes,
taking a first breath of the great air
around the bed. I look at you, you look
through the softly glowing rectangle of light
we remember will lead us to the living room.
Get up. No one has to say it. We move
from darkness into an orange-yellow glow,
toward a copper lamp hanging from the ceiling.
If ever we move from here, this room,
this light, this time of waking up with you,
not conscious or intelligible, is what
I want to bring with us to the next world.
Walking behind I feel the swish of your nightgown
between us, it moves with your rhythm, and so what
if I have a place to go in less than an hour.
We have two cups of tea, a bedside stand
for them to sit on while we undress again.

Undressing again, I stare at your breasts
against the flat, gray-blue of sky
there in the window now. Your shapes, my own,
we lie down, closing our eyes into the shapeless
ocean of movement under the sheet, not sleep,
not rest or conversation, only the wash
and wish of arms lightly over shoulders, hands
following a smoothness down, the belly, thighs
tightening, opening, tightening, opening.

james clark anderson

THE SURGE

Maybe it is the shyness of the pride
he has when he puts my hand down to feel
the hardness of his cock I hadn't tried

by any conscious gesture to raise,
yet it rose for my soft presence in the bed:
there was nothing I did to earn its praise

but be alive next to it. Maybe it is
the softness of want beneath his delight
at his body going on without his . . .

his will, really, his instructions . . . that
surges inside me as a sort of surrender
to the fact that I am, that I was made, that

there is nothing I need do to please but be.
To do nothing but be, and thus be wanted:
so, this is love. *Look what happened*, he says as he

watches my hand draw out what it did not raise,
purpled in sleep. The surge inside me must
come from inside me, where the world lies,

just as the prick stiffened to amaze us
came from a rising inside him. The blessing
we feel is knowing that *out there* is nothing.
The world inside us has come to praise us.

molly peacock

THE PLEASURE OF FEELING INSIDE YOUR BODY

the pleasure of feeling inside your body
and your body and your body and your mind
such ecstasy that has not been felt before
as though you were waves rising and falling
the motion of the sea
as though you were a bird
flying swiftly over the ocean
the moon in the background
a symbol of peace and serenity
as though ecstasy had been achieved
for the first time in a long memory
and one who could not play music
became a musician
a trumpeter a guitarist a pianist
a woman whose fingers played the harp
and became an instrument
or whose lips made the lips of the horn
melt and bend

as though woman became man
experiencing the pleasure of woman
coming over and over again
touching the center of her existence
and knowing the warmth of the sun
the fire of the moon

the rhythm of summer cicadas
butterflies bluejays
japanese beetles aglow like a jewel
emerald dazzling
fluttering frightening

rochelle lynn holt

SEA INSIDE THE SEA

How well he knows he must lift out
the desolate Buddha, unfurl the scroll
raked anciently with its dragon's claw
of waiting. Silk banner embossed
with the myriad invigorations of the blood
pulling the tide toward us
until our bodies don't hoard eternity
but are spun through with a darting vehemence,
until the abundant thing made of us spikes free
of even its ripening, that moan of white fingers at a depth
that strips the gears of the soul.

I lick salt of him from under his eyes,
from the side of the face. Prise open each wave
in its rising, in its mouth-to-breast-to-groin.
A velvet motionlessness where the halo
lingers as if between two endless afternoons
in which a round presence, most quiet and
most unquiet, is tended. Because love
has decided and made a place of us.
Has once again asked its boldest question
as an answer.

We are the lucidity of salt, jealous
even of its craving. It follows
its thirst with its neck outstretched
so like the shy deer
who come down from the mountain.
They run their quick tongues
over the wet ribbons of seaweed. But we are so far inside
the body-ness of the body, that the hieroglyphics of their
    hoofprints
inscribe the many-paired lips of the sea's cave mouth
which, even now, drinks wave onto wave.

We are overspent into awakening like the pinched scent
of aniseed that carries its sex
as a bruising. He lifts himself like an answer
in which love, as it knows not to speak
but is many-chasmed, says, "Ask me. Ask me
anything." Again, his palm passes over
the mute belly, passes and repasses.
Her gold and silver rings in a heap
on the headboard. His naked hand. Hers
more naked. The sea turned back nightlong
by the blackened tide of her hair
across no shore.

    tess gallagher

PALMS

the trees make their mark on the sky
your name is on my breath
I want to kneel, feel my knees press
into the earth, very close
the roots of trees
are like ancient, strong fingers

a bird lifts into the evening sky
another flies below
then, as if moved by the same wing
they glide to rest on the same branch

the whorls and lines across old trees
make rare palms against the sky
signal a secret language
a silence older than love

following the flight of birds
we see the sky more clearly
how horizon may join two worlds
the way a bird joins the sky
the way trees join the earth
the way we join each other

your fingers are brown and strong
like earth, like trees
when you pull me to you
I move, rising and rooted
the strength of earth below
above, the free stretch of sky

june sylvester

PLEASURE

I've dimmed the lights low,
smoothed your eyelids still,

humming as I work, touching you
until time fades, falls away.

Like a slow blues, I glide —
hands over nape and neck,

strokes easy, never sudden,
a fingertip rhythm beckoning

pleasure out from under, bringing
peace to tired shoulders, blades

surrendering to pressure,
touch upon touch, my palms

tracing muscles, ribs, belly,
the demure pubic triangle.

I don't stop my hands
from touching every region:

assiduous calves, toes,
tentative penis cradled

by my palm, shy testicles
coaxed by my tongue. Never

thought healing could be
this easy, bodies freed

from scrutiny, that tyranny
suspended for the pleasure

we gain in simplest movement:
hands cradling breasts,

your lips pursed around
a single stiffening nipple.

allison joseph

FAR IN

Full stop. Let's not
do anything. Wait
for what is spreading
underneath the skin,
the limit on this
only how much ripeness
we can stand. Full
stop. Are you
a woman, am I a man,
which one of us is fuller
with the other? Something
in pleasure is just
out of ken, floats
like a lily on a lake
that deepens farther in.

rachel loden

ENVOI: WAKING AFTER SNOW

When did we drift into each other's arms?
Snow, blue as morning, shakes down
in the branches, not a breath among them.
I can't tell if we're one body or two.
As soon as he's settled, the redbird puffs up
his whole heart to the cold. Don't move.

david baker

OLD MOON WITH HER YOUTH IN HER ARMS

We lie before the fire after love,
my body cupped to capture rays of warmth
on bare, shivering skin. From behind
in the dark, you trace the curve of light
on my limbs, describing my body as an ark
full of booty. I smile at your hyperbole.
I am years past fullness, your wife for
more than half my life. Our sons, born
in a term of fuller flesh, are each day
more of the world and less of us. At times,
alone in the dark, I feel myself shrink
in a gathering emptiness — not a laden ark,
but a waning crescent moon, eclipsed
by my own growing history.
                                        Still,
tonight, your voice reaching from behind
tethers my past to my visible part, and
your hand stroking my back, my thigh,
wraps fresh desires about my flesh. So,
lightly slung in the rounding shape
of my life, I trust to sleep.

gale swiontkowski

DEAD STILL

Now, with your palms on the blades of my shoulders,
Let us embrace:
Let there be only your lips' breath on my face,
Only, behind our backs, the plunge of rollers.

Our backs, which like two shells in moonlight shine,
Are shut behind us now;
We lie here huddled, listening brow to brow,
Like life's twin formula or double sign.

In folly's world-wide wind
Our shoulders shield from the weather
The calm we now beget together,
Like a flame held between hand and hand.

Does each cell have a soul within it?
If so, fling open all your little doors,
And all your souls shall flutter like the linnet
In the cages of my pores.

Nothing is hidden that shall not be known.
Yet by no storm of scorn shall we
Be pried from this embrace, and left alone
Like muted shells forgetful of the sea.

Meanwhile, O load of stress and bother,
Lie on the shells of our backs in a great heap:
It will but press us closer, one to the other.

We are asleep.

> *andrei voznesensky*
> [translated from the Russian by *richard wilbur*]

YOU TOUCH ME

I like to look at you
asleep on your side, face
cradled by down soft pillow.
I like to read
you like a poem, slowly
attending to the detailed
lines about the eyes
slipping under lids, lips
pursed as if about to kiss.

In this, your nightly cruise,
you take leave
from port of day's
forgotten words meeting
off course to sail along
the sea of dark
through strings of island stars,
at the masthead bearing on
toward sun about to be
uncovered.

I like to see you stir
when into the small
cupped petal of your ear,

my whisper drifts:
touch me, touch me.
I like to watch you rise
as if some foreign tongue
you once spoke came
suddenly back to you, watch
you fix a course across
the sheeted light onto
the continent of my body.

andrena zawinski

MANON REASSURES HER LOVER

When I cannot sleep, I stroke you,
and like a napping cat that purrs
and stretches when touched, you linger
with pleasure on the edge of waking,
curling far into slumber. You know
that I am watching, you are safe.
Your skin is soft, smells fresh.

I love how your face is sculpted,
the drapes and furrows, how your cheek
laps over your forearm as you sleep.
I love how your skin moves under my hand,
the way it sags on the muscle and bone,
as the skin of a ripe peach
slips loose almost without the knife.

I have no hunger for young flesh,
unripe, firm but tasteless by comparison.
You are still at the very peak
of ripeness, sweet, with the tang
that quenches thirst. I would like
to take a gentle bite from your shoulder,
golden in the faint light from the window.

martha elizabeth

YOU BRING ME BACK

You bring me back
with a smell
a shape
to my early pleasure.
Deep in the night
I climb the high
chair of your lap
and rest in sure
familiar dreams.

When I turn, you turn
and I become host
to your sleeping
body, your naked body.
Kneading the flesh
aligning the bones
till morning arouses
a shape, a smell
and we turn to each other
in familiar pleasure.

patti tana

ENCOUNTER

Did you wake me?
Or I, you?

Perhaps it was the sneeze
I tried to muffle
In the billows of soft down
That float over us
Through cold winter nights.

The awakening was
A slow untangling
From the webs of dream.
Then passion took its own
Sweet time as well — at first
Beginning with gentle touch
But building rapidly
To fierce breathlessness
And final rushing cries.

An intensity of contact
That's always amazing
Beyond understanding.
How that cold room
Glowed with warmth.

rick fournier

BEDSIDE

Early dawn shows the maroon and tan shell
we found on the Gulf the day you were diving
and kicking fins through jade water. Luminous
pink in your hand and wide-eyed, spray and salt
and fish smell as we broke for air. The scent here

comes from potpourri, the gray pot your sister brought
from the north, on the wicker shelf we carried
in from the old house, and there's the chewed
stick we throw for the dog down the running
trail. That pine cone is from the gnarled

Ponderosa on the white knoll where we camped
and you watched the sweat drip down my arms
and our eyes glistened like the wet rocks.
Later I brought a chunk of lava shot with crystals
from New Jersey and the frayed journal, the fine

clock your birthday present, faint green lines
on black as the sky grays, as on how many
work mornings. Cough lozenges, my watch, torn
movie tickets: how many times we hugged
or slapped each other, laughing or came out

of the same meeting with tears streaming: how much
of my life is here, and how much of yours! The curve
of your waist as you turn toward me and crack
your eyes open, dark lashes against your cheeks.
I fold my arms around you and embrace

the quality of your smile as you wake.
The years behind you bathed in dawn.

clive matson

THE KNOWING

Afterwards, when we have slept, paradise-
comaed, and woken, we lie a long time
looking at each other.
I do not know what he sees, but I see
eyes of surpassing tenderness
and calm, a calm like the dignity
of matter. I love the open ocean
blue-gray-green of his iris, I love
the curve of it against the white,
that curve the sight of what has caused me
to come, when he's quite still, deep
inside me. I have never seen a curve
like that, except the earth from outer
space. I don't know where he got
his kindness without self-regard,
almost without self, and yet
he chose one woman, instead of the others.
By knowing him, I get to know
the purity of the animal
which mates for life. Sometimes he is slightly
smiling, but mostly he just gazes at me gazing,
his entire face lit. I love
to see it change if I cry — there is no worry,
no pity, a graver radiance. If we
are on our backs, side by side,

with our faces turned fully to face each other,
I can hear a tear from my lower eye
hit the sheet, as if it is an early day on earth,
and then the upper eye's tears
braid and sluice down through the lower eyebrow
like the invention of farming, irrigation,
    a non-nomadic people.
I am so lucky that I can know him.
This is the only way to know him.
I am the only one who knows him.
When I wake again, he is still looking at me,
as if he is eternal. For an hour
we wake and doze, and slowly I know
that though we are sated, though we are hardly
touching, this is the coming the other
brought us to the edge of — we are entering,
deeper and deeper, gaze by gaze,
this place beyond the other places,
beyond the body itself, we are making
love.

sharon olds

CHAPTER FIVE

graceful transformations

WATERING THE NEW LAWN

It took us both to water the new lawn,
our nozzles splashing life on the warm seeds
in peat mossed dust, desperate for water and sun.

Milky diamonds dangled in strips of beads
from our hoses as we danced from the edges
toward each other in the crotch of the yard.

We took positions near each other, nudged
our streams slowly back and forth, saturating
each waiting seed, with practiced rhythms

repeated a thousand times, lovers making
life grow. This could be our last lawn, we knew,
and aged expertise had taught us to take our sweet time.

michael s. smith

MARRIED LOVE

You and I
Have so much love,
That it
Burns like a fire,
In which we bake a lump of clay
Molded into a figure of you
And a figure of me.
Then we take both of them,
And break them into pieces,
And mix the pieces with water,
And mold again a figure of you,
And a figure of me.
I am in your clay.
You are in my clay.
In life we share a single quilt.
In death we will share one coffin.

> *kuan tao shêng*
> [translated from the Chinese by
> *kenneth rexroth* and *ling chung*]

PRAISE

In my hands your
body is a hymnal
open to the familiar
page of praise. I
sing you in the ancient
rhythm that brought
us all here to make
what we will of
this world, I sing
you in tongues and
in silent awe of our
loving, certain only
of imminent separation.

anne k. smith

FOREPLAY

It starts in the morning
when I wake up
as you hold me
and ask me how I slept.

It starts at breakfast
when you tell me
what you'll be doing at work
and where you can be reached.

It's how sweetly you kiss me
when you leave
and it continues during the day
when you call just to say hello.

It's when you come home
and hug me
and tell me you've missed me
and ask me about my day.

It goes on during dinner
when we listen to each other
and you hold my hand
as we share our thoughts.

And when we finally go to bed
I am ready to make love.

natasha josefowitz

ORCHESTRATION

Your hip replacement mended,
my back pain abated,
our bed that seemed too small
has re-expanded.
As you lie gently next to me,
your good-night embrace
strikes a chord that becomes
the prelude.

Gingerly, sedately,
we respond to melodic memories
from a former, unfettered age;
and imagination becomes
the grandparent of two-part invention.
Subtlety and innuendo
compose the music of mature love
that orchestrates enjoyment
and unites the musicians
in soul-vibrating harmony.

jane mayes

THE VERY FLOOR OF OUR EXISTENCE

The very floor of our existence as a couple
a floor, a stage, our bed.
It is here where the white-haired lover under
a ceiling of eleven glow-in-the-dark stars,
in that dark of having performed these rituals
a decade short of fifty years,
finds me in search of him.
Long ago we ceased buying each other bed clothes
at Christmas. Adam and Eve, our parents,
knew better. Bed uncovers the distances day imposes.
Older people, crystallized and sweetened like honey
left in some jar on a shelf, by this intercourse of bee
to flower, our massages, messages shared
under the sanctuary of a coverlet. Your hands
coax music from the ivory of a grand piano,
athletic hands that turned to building fences,
documenting lives once lived.
Mine have kneaded bread, have shaped the mysteries
around us into words, our signatures on skin,
have soothed the foreheads of fevered children.
Over the small of your back, furled like a flag, a percale
border of robin's egg blue, and peach flowers
    strewn in a pattern
embracing those shoulders you complain
    are not quite broad enough

now bending with age. When the strong lines down your
    face meet
the crosshatches under and around my eyes,
you say, "Did you remember to bring anything?"
Then our stacked bellies tremble in tandem,
    the rippling of chuckles felt,
a laughter filling the bed room, as I respond with the
    usual, "No."

june billings safford

YOUR BODY GLISTENS FROM THE BATH

in the mirror in front of me
my hands on you
your hands reach back
as we stand dripping
slippery and delicious
our tongues and we
begin again
the long slow dance
we have perfected
like pilgrims returning
home again
to the promised land

charles rossiter

MIDDLE AGE

Crashing down mossy walls
the water foams in a fierce whirlpool.
Away from the main current we wait
a chilled pool, our surface still
till we are sucked into the turbulence
coming together in that seductive swirl

and after we emerge, the roar
of the water subsiding, the breeze cooling
too soon we sink back, and wait.

arlene l. mandell

AND THIS IS SO

Yours is the only body
I have known.
Here have I found my realization
and my renewing,
and here in the true spreading
of you
I have sown sons and daughters
born strong and bearing
our love.

I have lain rested in you
and felt the constancy of ebbing heat
raised in flesh passion.

My lips have sensed the promise
of no other breasts, my hands
have stroked no other generous thighs,
my heart has sought no other direction.

joseph h. ball

OF GRAVITY & ANGELS

And suddenly, again,
I want the long road of your thigh
under my hand, your well-travelled thigh,
your salt-slicked & come-slicked thigh,
and I want the taste of you, slaking,
under my tongue (that place of riding desire,
my tongue) and I want
all the unnameable, soft, and yielding places,
belly & neck & the place wings would rise from
if we were angels,
and we are, and I want the rising regions of you
shoulder & cock & tongue & breathing &
suddenness of you
opening
all fontanel, all desire, the whole thing beginning
for the first time again, the first,
until I wonder then how is it
we even know which part we are,
even know the ground that lifts us, raucous,
out of ourselves,
as the rising sound of a summer dawn
when all of it joins in.

jane hirshfield

WE TAKE THE NEW YOUNG COUPLE OUT TO DINNER

> *"A more complete human being is a*
> *human being who is more completely*
> *bestial."*
>
> — NIETZSCHE

They go at it in the backseat of our car,
then on into the restaurant,
and later out on the sidewalk,
their snatching hands all over each other
so we will see the heat flashing between them
like the neon in a splashy marquee
above a theater they would have us enter
a blunted old-married couple,
the wistful audience
before their flickering screen.

    What they would never think is
how we are thinking just now
of monkey island at the zoo,
the meticulous chimps
fingering one another's pelts,
browsing for fleas, the lone baboon
masturbating to beat the band.

    And still at it
when we say our tactful goodnights,
what they would never think is

how we will unlock the doors
of our own modest house
and with you hard
behind me, your hands clasping
my swaying hips,
feel our way, breathless
through the jungle dark.

carol tufts

SPRINGTIME AT TWILIGHT

We must have done this thousands of times
In twenty years of marriage, everything
In its place, tucked in neatly at the seams,
Laid back but lustful as first bursts of Spring.

We have our times together now, routines
And obligations ingrained as wrinkled brows;
But sometimes fresh surprising passion returns
Like February crocuses bright mornings arouse.

I hold your hair entwined in my fingers
And snuggle into all your cavities
And curves, abhorring any open space
Between us. Breathing deeply, like singers,
Our practiced rhythm makes sweet harmonies
And I'm awed by the glow on your close-up face.

michael s. smith

TWIN FLAMES

Embers of night flare up afresh
when you ignite the morning in my arms
and kindle the familiar hearth of love

Year after year we have warmed our lives
around the mystery of mutual fire
that heats our domain of risk and rapture

Whenever scorched   however scarred
we hearten   heal   reconflagrate
Twin flames ever   in blissful blaze

james broughton

OUR LOVE

Our love is the autumn languish
days draw lazy and pungent,
ripe fruit, leaf susurration
prelude to fugue
our shoulders fit; our bellies
our liquors merge slowly —
we lie so close
our hearts beat angels.

jo nelson

PLACE SETTING

Hold me

let me lay my head
in that special spot
on your chest
beneath your chin
where I fit so well.

johari m. rashad

ADAGIO AT TWILIGHT

Why
as the tips of the petals curl and darken does
the rose grow yet more rare

               and why do the years
so adorn your loveliness?

Why
as I gaze at you asleep

           and drink your breath
and touch the naked beauty of your soul
do tears come to my eyes?

Why old friend

          does each new line on your face
pluck with ravenous fingers at my heart
and strike these chords of longing?

And what of the music flaming in my blood
and what of my swollen flesh?

     john carter

NOSTALGIA

we begin kissing
around eleven
by noon
we're naked
it's been a long time
but we remember
the sweep of history
around us
like an envelope
of radiant heat
our image
in the mirror
shines with such
sweet melancholy
we fall again
into each other
where it is warm
and years ago
and the world
outside these walls
has not yet
been imagined

charles rossiter

DECADE

When you came, you were like red wine and honey,
And the taste of you burnt my mouth with its sweetness.
Now you are like morning bread,
Smooth and pleasant.
I hardly taste you at all for I know your savour,
But I am completely nourished.

amy lowell

RETURN

Return often and take me,
beloved sensation, return and take me
when the memory of the body awakens,
and old desire again runs through the blood;
when the lips and the skin remember,
and the hands feel as if they touch again.

Return often and take me at night,
when the lips and the skin remember . . .

> *c. p. cavafy*
> [translated by *rae dalven*]

VANISHING POINT

Staring, you look for clues.
Where is the evidence, the proof.

In your stare I watch myself gazing,
enamored, at skylines,
or blinded by a pine cone in hand.

Love, when it stays, is traceless.
Whose hand stretched first offering is no matter.
The bodies press together in their many ways.

The one coarse piece of cloth drapes us both
and softens on the curves of our bodies
and our lives fit well.

When two people walk far enough into the distance
they merge.

gary metras

PERMISSION ACKNOWLEDGMENTS

Grateful acknowledgment is made to poets who contributed unpublished and previously published works for this collection. Unless specifically noted otherwise, copyright of the poems is held by the individual poets. Thanks also are due to the following poets, publications and publishers for permission to reprint the copyrighted materials listed below:

DEBORAH ABBOTT: "All Day at Work," from *Erotic by Nature: A Celebration of Life, Love and Our Wonderful Bodies* by David Steinberg (Santa Cruz, CA: Down There Press/Red Alder Books, 1988), p. 160. Copyright © 1988 by Deborah Abbott. Reprinted with the permission of Down There Press/Red Alder Books.

KIM ADDONIZIO: "Alone in Your House," from *The Philosopher's Club* by Kim Addonizio (Brockport, NY: BOA Editions, Ltd., 1994). Copyright © 1994 by Kim Addonizio. Reprinted with the permission of BOA Editions, Ltd.

JAMES CLARK ANDERSON: "Waking Up Twice," appeared in *Yellow Silk: Journal of Erotic Arts*, (Albany, CA: Yellow Silk Publications), vol. 7, Fall/Winter 1991, p. 9. Copyright © 1991 by James Clark Anderson. Reprinted by permission of the poet and Yellow Silk Publications.

ACKNOWLEDGMENTS

Without the help of some remarkable people, my dream of this anthology would never have become a reality. My dear friend and fellow author, Suzie Boss, conducted early research for the book, then later did a beautiful job of helping to craft the introduction. I also am grateful to Molly Fisk who assisted me with research, selection, editing, and organization of the early manuscript.

Many thanks go to Molly Peacock, a gifted poet, for her ideas, enthusiasm, and invaluable involvement throughout many stages of this project. In addition, I am indebted to the following poets, writers, and publishers for providing helpful guidance and encouragement: Robert Grudin, Micha Grudin, Garrett Hongo, Elizabeth Claman, David Steinberg, Kim Stafford, Suzanne Jennings, David Bonanno of *The American Poetry Review*, Stephen Corey of *The Georgia Review*, and Lily Pond of *Yellow Silk* magazine. Two publications, *Poet and Writer's Magazine* and *The Loft*, helped me attract submissions from talented poets across the country.

I want to thank many poets who sent me their very

personal, heartfelt poems for consideration. Although space prevented me from including all their work, it was wonderful to receive so much support for the intent and design of the collection from so many people. I also am grateful to the poets whose excellent works appear in the collection for their often generous contributions in granting me permission to publish.

Sincere thanks go to Sequoia Lundy, Norma Ragsdale, and Rick Nelson for reading the manuscript and offering input for trimming the number of selections for the collection.

I am deeply indebted to my literary agent, Felicia Eth. She maintained a steadfast belief in this book throughout its many phases. Felicia's warmth and guidance helped nurture the project and find the right publisher for the collection. I am especially grateful she understands and actively supports my goals in the area of sex education and healing.

Similarly, I feel incredibly lucky to have the opportunity to work with socially conscious and talented individuals at New World Library. I want to thank publisher Marc Allen for recognizing the value of the collection and sharing my vision. Becky Benenate, my amazing editor, provided a wealth of enthusiasm, creativity, wisdom, and technical effort in transforming the collection into its present gift book form. I also would like to thank Munro Magruder, the marketing director, for his friendly support and ideas.

I also am deeply grateful to my teenage children, Cara

and Jules, for their understanding and patience during those times when this project required special attention.

And finally, I want to thank my incredible husband, Larry Maltz. He provided countless hours of assistance in evaluating poems and securing permissions, and supplied an abundance of emotional support and care on the home front. Larry's passionate love is the true inspiration for this book. For it is through him, and with him, that I have come to know personally the beauty and rewards of healthy sexual intimacy.

ABOUT THE EDITOR

Wendy Maltz, M.S.W., is a nationally recognized psychotherapist and lecturer on healthy sexuality and sexual healing. She is author of *The Sexual Healing Journey: A Guide for Survivors of Sexual Abuse* (1992), coauthor of *In the Garden of Desire: The Intimate World of Women's Sexual Fantasies* (1997), and coauthor of *Incest and Sexuality: A Guide to Understanding and Healing* (1987). Wendy has written and narrated two video productions, "Partners in Healing" and "Relearning Touch Techniques," for couples healing the intimate repercussions of sexual abuse and addiction. She is codirector, with her husband Larry, of Maltz Counseling Associates and lives in Eugene, Oregon. Her website is www.healthysex.com.

ABOUT THE COVER PHOTOGRAPHER

Photographer Paul Dahlquist was born in 1929 in Teaneck, New Jersey. He received his MFA from the University of Washington in 1958. He taught high school in Washington from 1960 until he retired in 1985. The challenge to explore the gift of passion, often maligned, misunderstood, and repressed, is important to Dahlquist. He lives in Portland, OR.

Cover photograph as originally taken

New World Library is dedicated to publishing
books and cassettes that inspire and challenge us
to improve the quality of our lives and our world.

For a catalog of our fine books
and cassettes contact:

New World Library
14 Pamaron Way
Novato, California 94949

Phone: (415) 884-2100
Fax: (415) 884-2199
Or call toll-free: (800) 972-6657
Catalog requests: Ext.50
Ordering: Ext. 52

E-mail: escort@nwlib.com
www.newworldlibrary.com